Literary Villages of London

Also in this series:

Literary Cafés of Paris
  by Noël Riley Fitch

Literary Neighborhoods of New York
  by Marcia Leisner

LITERARY
VILLAGES
OF
LONDON

Luree Miller

STARRHILL PRESS
Washington & Philadelphia

Starrhill Press, publisher
P.O. Box 32342
Washington, D.C. 20007
(202) 686-6703

Copyright © 1989 by Luree Miller.
All rights reserved.

Illustrations by Jonel Sofian.
Maps by Deb Norman.

Library of Congress Cataloging in Publication Data

Miller, Luree.
    Literary villages of London / Luree Miller.—1st ed.
        p.   cm.
    Bibliography: p.
    Includes index.
    ISBN 0-913515-41-8 : $7.95
    1. Literary landmarks—England—London—Guide-books. 2. English 83
literature—England—London—History and criticism. 3. Authors,
English—Homes and haunts—England—London—Guide-books. 4. London
(England) in literature. 5. London (England)—Description—1981- -
-Guide- books. 6. London (England)—Intellectual life. I. Title.
PR110.L6M55   1989
914.21'04858—dc19
                                                  88-36889
                                                     CIP

Printed in the United States of America.
First edition
9 8 7 6 5 4 3 2 1

For Judy Hillelson and Dick Ehrlich,
who walked with me.

Contents

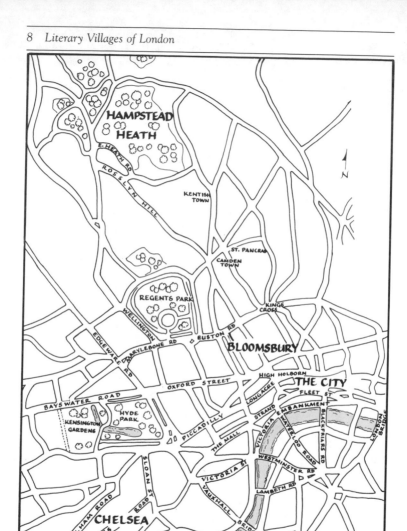

London

The Villages

By seeing London, I have seen as much of life as the world can show.
— Samuel Johnson, quoted by James Boswell

IF YOU THINK of London as a great patchwork of villages slowly stitched together through the centuries, you can sense why this metropolis has always been congenial to writers. Village life persists in the midst of urban sophistication.

For this informal, anecdotal guide, I have chosen Bloomsbury, Chelsea, the City and Hampstead as villages with the strongest literary associations. In these places writers lived in close enough clusters to reward the walker looking for literary landmarks.

Leaving out other villages was difficult. For six happy years I lived in Mayfair, where Henry James wrote *The Europeans* and *Daisy Miller,* and where William Thackeray set some of the most dramatic scenes in *Vanity Fair.* My children went to school in Marylebone, where Edward Lear lived, and came home along Sherlock Holmes's famous Baker Street. I walked to work down Wimpole Street past the site of Elizabeth Barrett's family home which she fled to elope with Robert Browning, her fiery poet lover. And I met friends for lunch in Soho, today an area of excellent restaurants favored by journalists, editors and publishers. Soho was where the poet, William Blake, was born. John Dryden and Samuel Coleridge lived there, as did Percy Shelley, when he was sent down from Oxford. Every corner of London echoes with literary allusions. It was hard to leave any out any landmark, but impossible to include them all.

Writers have always defined themselves and been defined by the places they lived. The original City of London, where the English language sprouted out of a medley of foreign tongues, has for more than seven centuries been the fertile center of English literature. When Chaucer, Shakespeare and Pepys referred to London, they meant that City contained within one square mile of Roman walls. As royal enclaves, villages, and speculative developments like Covent Garden and Bloomsbury sprang up outside the City walls, writers began to move farther afield, but not so far that they weren't still considered Londoners.

"You find no man, at all intellectual, who is willing to leave London," Dr. Johnson declared. "No, Sir, when a man is tired of London, he is tired of life; for there is in London all that life can afford."

In the 18th century when Dr. Johnson made his famous declaration, the heart of the writing life was around St Paul's Cathedral and up Fleet Street. But coffeehouses, where journalists and authors sought the stimulation of good conversation, were springing up outside the City, and London was fast becoming a larger concept. Writers could find cheaper digs, less noise and more healthful air in surrounding villages without really leaving London.

The City, often called the Square Mile, remains a separate administrative entity with its own Lord Mayor. It and the surrounding patchwork of villages have been sewn together by roads and the underground to make up Greater London. The seams scarcely show, but on close examination you'll find that each village has retained its distinctive character and is rich with its own literary associations.

Walking is the best way, it seems to me, to experience that strong sense of place that London writers convey. They walked. They knew their streets and the life in them. Portly Dr. Johnson, compiling his great dictionary, seldom strayed far from Fleet Street, for he found ample stimulation in the City. But other writers, more attuned to Nature, preferred to live in Hampstead, where they could stretch their legs on the open heath. "I met Wordsworth on Hampstead Heath this morning," John Keats wrote to a friend. When Robert Louis Stevenson stayed at Abernethy House in Hampstead, he declared it "the most delightful place for air and scenery" and said that he had been "all day, walking and strolling about the heath." In Chelsea, Thomas Carlyle lived near the Thames and made a point, in true English fashion, of taking a walk every afternoon from two to four. Charles Dickens prowled the lanes and alleys of Victorian London and left us a vivid picture of the city in that best and worst of times. And Virginia Woolf, Vanessa Bell, their family and friends all dashed from square to square visiting each other in Bloomsbury until they and the area became synonymous.

I have tried to route my four walks in these villages down footlanes and through courtyards, the way writers who lived there might have walked. London is crowded now with cars and buses, but by avoiding the main roads as much as possible, you get a feeling for what it was like before motor traffic. For centuries the city's din was composed of the clomp of horses' hooves and the shrill cries of street hawkers. But there were always havens of quiet

Sicilian Avenue, Bloomsbury

in secret gardens, small lanes and tree-filled squares. Much of this charm is still to be found in the gardens of the Inns of Court in the City, the side streets in Chelsea, the cobbled walks of Hampstead and the squares of Bloomsbury.

Each of these four villages has a focal point or place of pilgrimage worth visiting if you have neither the time nor inclination to take the walks I have mapped.

In Bloomsbury on Great Russell Street the **BRITISH MUSEUM** is stuffed with treasures for every taste. There the great, domed British Library Reading Room, essential to generations of writers, is on view to the public every hour on the hour from 11 a.m. to 4 p.m. Monday through Friday. Tickets are needed to use the Reading Room. They are given to those with a letter of recommendation and an acceptable reason for using the library. The museum is open 10 a.m. to 5 p.m. Monday through Saturday and 2:30 to 6 p.m. on Sunday.

In the other three villages the focal points are homes of writers. It is not just "frivolous curiousity," Virginia Woolf wrote, that compels us to visit "Johnson's house and Carlyle's house and Keats's house. We know them from their houses—it would seem to be a fact that writers stamp themselves upon their possessions more indelibly than other people." And they have, she added, "a faculty for housing themselves appropriately."

In Chelsea the house of **JANE AND THOMAS CARLYLE** at 5 Cheyne Row is open Wednesday through Friday, 11 a.m. to 1 p.m. and 2 to 6 p.m. or dusk if earlier and Sunday from 2 to 6 p.m. or dusk if earlier. Both Carlyles attracted a wide circle of distinguished contemporaries. The house, with Carlyle's "sound-proof" study, is restored and includes original furnishings and many personal items.

In the City, Dr. **SAMUEL JOHNSON**'s house, at 17 Gough Square, is open May through September, Monday through Saturday, 11 a.m. to 5:30 p.m., and October through April, Monday through Saturday, 11 a.m. to 5 p.m. Here, while writing essays that appeared in *The Rambler* every Tuesday and Saturday, the great lexicographer compiled the first complete dictionary of the English language. Its 41,000 entries were transcribed by a half-dozen scribes Johnson installed at long tables in the attic room.

In Hampstead, **JOHN KEATS**'s house, Wentworth Place, in Keats Grove, is open Monday through Saturday from 10 a.m. to 6 p.m. and Sundays 2 to 5 p.m. (times may change). Keats was in love with Fanny Brawne, the girl next door. He sent her notes and they became engaged. These notes, letters and other memorabilia of Keats and his friends are preserved in the house. It was in the lovely garden here that Keats heard a nightingale sing and was inspired to write his famous "Ode to a Nightingale."

These houses and others along the walks are designated by plaques. Blue plaques were instituted in the 1860s "to insure that the old haunts of London may be preserved from the ruthless hands of modern destroyers and improvers." They were not always successful and sometimes simply commemorate the sites of historic buildings. Other plaques have been put up by local boroughs or societies. Except for the three museum houses mentioned, all houses with plaques are private dwellings not open to the public.

In London it is not proper to stare at public figures. If you should glimpse a well-known writer—Margaret Drabble shopping in Hampstead or Tom Stoppard lunching in Chelsea—quickly glance back at this book. The villages described here are much favored by the literati, but I have not included the homes or haunts of any living writers.

When Henry James wrote, "Summer afternoon—summer afternoon; to me those have always been the two most beautiful words in the English language," he had probably looked out on rain in the morning. The island's unpredictable weather breeds hope, so don't let clouds keep you in. Just take a "brolly" at all times.

Since the underground is the easiest and quickest way to get around London, the walks start at tube stations. Whenever I join the crowds streaming down stairs into the stations, I think of World War II Londoners hurrying deep into these shelters as air raid sirens droned. Those who made it into the stations slept on the cold cement platforms and survived the bombings.

But if you feel claustrophobic in the underground and prefer to see where you are going, climb to the top deck of a bus and settle in the front (no smoking) seats for a wonderful view. For bus information call 222-1234. Tell them where you are and where you want to go. They will tell you what number bus to take, at what time, how much it will cost, and how long it will take to get to your destination.

Even though this guide has maps and suggested walks, it is written primarily to convey the atmosphere of these literary villages, whether you actually visit them or not.

If you do stroll around the villages, notice that there are comfortable teak benches with backs and arms everywhere—along the streets, in the squares, and on the heath. So, please sit down, on a London bench or in your own reading chair, and sample with me the anecdotes and lore about celebrated writers who brightened the history of these urbane but homey literary villages of London.

The City

The chief glory of every people arises from its authors.
                    – Samuel Johnson
                    Preface to *Dictionary*, 1755

THE CITY once was the nicest place to live in London, declared contemporary writer **JOHN BETJEMAN**, who was Britain's poet laureate from 1972 to 1984. But finally, the noise of lorries rumbling down the narrow streets before dawn drove him and many others out. Few residents remain in the City today. Businesses and banks predominate. But Betjeman, like legions of writers before him, had been attracted by the vitality and color of this square mile. The City is crisscrossed by tiny foot passages and twisting alleys, dotted with quiet churches and cozy pubs, and still abounds with Chaucerian characters. "It is really a village of about four hundred people who know each other," Betjeman wrote, "and whose word is their bond."

GEOFFREY CHAUCER was probably born in this colorful village about 1340. His father was a prominent citizen and prosperous vintner. Gossip in the pubs must have been juicy when Chaucer fought with a friar in Fleet Street. Though few details of his life are known, tradition generally accepts this one.

Chaucer often is called "The Father of English Literature." It was here in this crowded, noisy, smelly, bustling village that English writers began to find their voices in a vernacular that became a great world language. Chaucer was one of the earliest to write in the dialect of the City. But it would be another four hundred years until another villager, Dr. Johnson, compiled his *Dictionary*, which established standard spelling and meaning for the English language.

The popularity of Chaucer's best known work, *The Canterbury Tales*, hasn't flagged since the fourteenth century. The poet has characters from all strata of society gather at the Tabard Inn in a suburb of London to set off on a pilgrimage to the famous shrine of St. Thomas Becket in Canterbury cathedral. On the way they tell their tales, which vary from serious to comic, pious to profane. There is a fraudulent pardoner, a charming prioress, Chanticleer, the learned cock in an animal fable, and the bawdy wife of Bath, who laments, "Alas, alas, that ever love was sin."

Throughout his life Chaucer was a busy man of affairs as well as a writer. After several trips abroad on the king's business, one of them a secret mission to Florence, he was appointed Controller of Customs to the Port of London in 1374. He was given a house over Ald Gate on the City's eastern boundary and granted a pitcher of wine daily. In *The House of Fame*, a love-vision or dream, Chaucer describes himself, after a busy day at the Port of London, hurrying home finally to crawl into his bed with a book and candle to read into the early hours of morning.

Chaucer's fortunes rose and fell with the royal feuds, but in the last years of his life a comfortable pension from Richard II was renewed by Henry IV. In 1400 Chaucer died and was buried in Westminster Abbey, an unusual honor for a commoner. The later Poets' Corner in the Abbey was centered around Chaucer's tomb.

Like many sons of the rich or noble classes, Chaucer probably learned his Latin and French at the Inns of Court. There he would have received a solid, expensive general and legal education preparing him for a career at court. Shortly before Chaucer was born, law students had leased the Inner and Middle Temple buildings that formerly belonged to the Order of Knights Templars. These rooms and halls, known collectively as the Temple, are two of the four Inns of Court. Nearly six hundred years after Chaucer, the American novelist Sinclair Lewis took rooms in the Temple near the Knights Templars' round church to work on his novel *Arrowsmith*. The setting reminded him of an American college campus.

Today the Inns of Courts are mostly law offices, but from medieval times through the nineteenth century they contained a lively mix of students and would-be students. Women keeping assignations in the Temple donned masks and drew their hoods about their faces to slip up the staircases. Parties, plays and feast days were celebrated in the rooms, halls and gardens. Maps on the walls of the Temple buildings have long lists of the famous, including literary figures, who have lived here, and they note many literary associations. Shakespeare's *Twelfth Night* was performed in 1601 for Queen Elizabeth in Middle Temple Hall. Dr. Johnson's Buildings on either side of Inner Temple Lane are named in memory of his residence from 1760 to 1765. **CHARLES LAMB,** essayist and author of the children's classic, *Tales From Shakespeare*, was born in the Temple at No. 2 Crown Row in 1775. In the gardens a fountain commemorates him. Beside it is a stone figure of a boy clasping a book with an inscription from Lamb: "Lawyers were children once."

WILLIAM SHAKESPEARE suggested killing all lawyers in one of his first plays, *King Henry, VI* Part II. He was a country lad in his early twenties and just one generation away from the soil when he drifted to London and a life in theater. He had married at eighteen and had a daughter six months later. But he was not unlearned. In the free grammar school of Stratford-upon-Avon, the market town where he was born in 1564, Shakespeare had studied Latin from six in the morning until five in the evening with a two-hour lunch break. In winter, school opened an hour later which cut the students' day from nine hours to eight.

In 1587, the probable year that Shakespeare came to the City, Queen Elizabeth had been ruling for twenty-eight years. It was the fateful year when the wily and magnificent Elizabeth, after years of court intrigue, had her great rival for the throne of England, Mary, Queen of Scots, beheaded. Shakespeare was twenty-three years old. Power, succession and loyalty were topics of the day, and he reflected these concerns in his historical plays.

According to Shakespeare, lines were drawn in the Temple for the War of the Roses, England's bloody civil conflict between the Houses of York and Lancaster. Richard Plantagenet and the Earls of Somerset, Suffolk and Warwick start to argue and Suffolk says, in *Henry VI* Part I, "Within the Temple-hall we were too loud; / The garden here is more convenient." The nobles then repair to the garden. Richard Plantagenet plucks a white rose for the House of York, Somerset a red rose for the House of Lancaster. After parrying some hot words, they part with Warwick saying sadly,

> And here I prophecy: this brawl to-day,
> Grown to this faction, in the Temple-garden,
> Shall send, between the red rose and the white
> A thousand souls to death and deadly night.

Sometime between 1587 and 1592 Shakespeare joined an acting company that played at the Rose Theatre. There his first play about Henry VI drew in the biggest crowds and made the most money of the entire season. An estimated ten thousand people came to see it. But the city fathers were uneasy about playhouses, fearing they would attract unruly elements and perhaps spread the plague. Therefore, they ruled, all theaters must stand outside the City boundaries. Bubonic plague was a constant threat in the City. It was virulent in 1592, and by September 1593 as many as one thousand Londoners were dying each week. The City Constable sealed plague-stricken houses and wrote on the doors, "Lord have mercy on us." Friar John in *Romeo and Juliet* alludes to the same practice in Verona:

> . . . . the searchers of the town,
> Suspecting that we both were in a house
> Where the infectious pestilence did reign,
> Seal'd up the doors, and would not let us forth;

But the rich and reckless young gentlemen from the Inns of Court continued to flock to the theaters and mingle with landless actors and playwrights. The Earl of Southhampton, who learned his law and manners at the Inns of Court, became the patron of actor and writer William Shakespeare, son of a provincial tradesman. Shakespeare dedicated his sonnets and two long poems, "Venus and Adonis" and "The Rape of Lucrece," to the earl. What their relationship was and how their social worlds overlapped remains a great literary mystery.

Shakespeare lodged for a while in Silver Street and later bought a house in Blackfriars. In the fifteen to twenty years that he was active in London theaters, Shakespeare wrote thirty-eight plays, or about two a year. His contemporaries recognized his genius and he prospered financially. However his father, John Shakespeare, fell on hard times and piled up debts. Presumably his son bailed him out because by 1596 an application to the heralds for a family coat of arms was granted John. A visitor to his glove shop remembered him as "a merry-cheekt old man always ready to crack a jest with his son."

Shakespeare was more a country than a city man. He kept close ties with Stratford, and his wife and family remained there all the years he lived in London. About 1610 he settled with them in Stratford's most substantial house with a fine garden and a farm nearby, but in 1613 he bought the Blackfriars house to stay in when he came up to London. The summer of that year his beloved Globe Theatre burned to the ground. Shakespeare had helped build and was part owner of this actor's dream theater, with its jutting apron, musicians' gallery and trapdoor, on the south bank of the Thames. Countless times he had hailed a boat-taxi or crossed London bridge (adorned with severed heads) to direct or act in his own plays. Shakespeare and his old crony, playwright **BEN JONSON**, were drinking together when Shakespeare caught the fever that caused his death in 1616. He and Ben may have been reminiscing over a glass of ale about the glorious days when they helped establish the theater as an enduring feature of London life. "All the world's a stage," was the motto of the Globe. In his plays Shakespeare showed us ourselves, camouflaged as characters on that world stage, and he elevated drama to an art that has never been equaled in English.

One of the favorite walks of **SAMUEL PEPYS** was to the Temple. Pepys was an incomparable diarist who chronicled a decade of seventeenth-century London life in rich detail. "A most agreeable place," he wrote of the Temple. "You quit all the hurry and bustle of the City in Fleet Street and the Strand, and all at once find yourself in a pleasant academical retreat. You see good convenient buildings, handsome walks, you view the silver Thames. You are shaded by venerable trees."

Samuel Pepys was born in Salisbury Court, Fleet Street, in 1632 and baptized in nearby St. Bride's Church. Very much a man of the City, Pepys soon rose to eminence as a civil servant, a Member of Parliament and Secretary of the Admiralty. Incorruptible, indefatigable and assiduous to detail, Pepys is credited with reforming the British Navy and establishing its great tradition of administrative discipline and service.

At the same time Pepys struggled to discipline himself. "Thanks be to God, since my leaving drinking of wine," he wrote, "I do find myself much better, and do mind my business better, and do spend less money, and less time lost in idle company."

Pepys was twenty-seven when he began his famous diary which he wrote in shorthand until his eyes began to fail him when he was thirty-six. His sharp eye for detail and his understanding of the complexities of the human heart make his diary a lively work of art. And his unsparing record of his own shortcomings endears him to readers. He loved his French-born wife but was an incorrigible philanderer: "Anon comes home my wife from Brampton, not looked for till Saturdy, which will hinder me of a little pleasure, but I am glad of her coming."

Pepys lived through the Great Plague of 1665, recording in his diary that "discourse in the street, is of death, and nothing else."

The next year he watched the Great Fire from his official residence in the navy office in Seething Lane, now named Pepys Street. The fire broke out at midnight, September 2, 1666, at the house of the king's baker in Pudding Lane. There had been a drought. Water was scarce. People were slow to act. High winds swept the flames down the narrow lanes of wood and plaster houses. Sparks ignited the thatched roofs. "The houses so very thick thereabouts," Pepys wrote, "and full of matter for burning, as pitch and tar, in Thames Street, and warehouses of oil, and wines, and brandy." People fled to the river. "Poor people," said Pepys, "staying in their houses as long as till the very fire touched them, then running into boats, or clambering from one pair of stairs by the waterside, to another. And among other things the poor pigeons, I perceive, were loath to leave their houses, but hovered about the windows and balconies, till they burned their wings and fell down."

Pepys wept to see his beloved City burn. But he saved the navy office and gave us an eye-witness account not only of the great tragedy but a picture of seventeenth-century life that remains one of the great works of English literature.

London, of course, rose from the ashes and continued to be a magnet for writers. In March 1737 two young friends burning with ambition rode together from Birmingham to storm the City. One was an actor, the other a writer. Both were geniuses. David Garrick, the actor, soon became famous. For SAMUEL JOHNSON, poet, critic, essayist, lexicographer and the greatest clubman of the eighteenth century, the struggle was longer and harder. But eventually his fame was greater. No English writer other than Shakespeare has remained better known or more widely quoted than Dr. Samuel Johnson.

A tall, powerfully built man, blind in one eye and with very poor sight in the other, Johnson struggled against poverty most of his life. He was born in Lichfield, Staffordshire, in 1709. Sickly as a child, Johnson fought ill health and bouts of melancholia all his life. A firm exponent of common sense and rationality he devised various stratagems to jolt himself out of his depressions. In his youth he forced himself to take long, demanding walks; in later years he organized clubs for conviviality and good conversation.

As a boy in his father's bookshop, Johnson read voraciously "with the instincts of an incipient scholar." Somehow, in spite of his family's dire poverty, he entered Oxford but was forced to leave after a year for lack of funds. When he went to London his journalistic abilities were quickly appreciated by editors of papers and periodicals, but he was never well paid. In 1738 he published his first substantial poem, a protest against political corruption titled "London." With characteristic wit he warns against the danger of the City streets:

> Their ambush here relentless ruffians lay,
>   And here the fell attorney prowls for prey;
> Here falling houses thunder on your head,
>   And here a female atheist talks you dead.

Despite the dangers of London, Johnson brought his wife from Birmingham. She was his "beloved Tetty," a former widow twenty years his senior to whom Johnson was devoted. They lived in the tall brick house in Gough Street, one of Johnson's many residences in London, while he worked on his remarkable dictionary. A syndicate of booksellers had approached Johnson for this pioneer work, and he signed a contract with them in 1746. The *Dictionary of the English Language* took eight years to complete and yielded him little profit. In it he defined more than forty thousand words and he illustrated their usage with over one hundred thousand quotations drawn from his prodigious reading.

During the time he was working on the *Dictionary*, Johnson had to write reviews and essays for periodicals to make ends meet. In the evenings of one week he dashed off his philosophical romance, *Rasselas*, to pay his mother's funeral expenses. It was his only work that achieved immediate popularity.

Johnson was a moralist with a strong sense of responsibility. He believed a writer's duty was to make the world better, though he phrased it less severely when he wrote, "The only end of writing is to enable the readers better to enjoy life or better to endure it." Johnson's many friends and admirers testified that this essentially lonely and melancholy man was able to lift their spirits. "He cleared my mind," said Sir Joshua Reynolds, "of a great deal of rubbish." From the memoirs of writers Fanny Burney and Mrs. Thrale, as well as Johnson's famous biographer, **JAMES BOSWELL**, we know he was a deeply compassionate man and a brilliant conversationalist.

Dr. Samuel Johnson's house in Gough Square

After Tetty died, in 1752, Johnson moved to Staple Inn and spent even more time in the popular London coffeehouses. He had told Boswell that a man might live very cheaply in the City if he frequented them. One could live in a garret, said Johnson, and reply if asked where he lodged, "Sir, I am to be found at such a place," naming his favorite coffeehouse. Boswell added Johnson's advice that, "For spending threepence in a coffee-house, you may be for hours in very good company. You may dine for sixpence, you may breakfast on bread and milk, and you may [go without] supper."

Boswell came to London from Scotland, intent on meeting famous men particularly Dr. Johnson. "I had learnt," said Boswell, "that his place of frequent resort was the Mitre Tavern, in Fleet Street, where he loved to sit up late, and I begged I might be allowed to pass an evening with him there soon." Legend says that the Cheshire Cheese, just off Fleet Street, was another favorite haunt of Johnson's. An American, CYRUS JAY, perpetuated that tradition in his book, *The Law: What I Have Seen, What I Have Heard, and What I Have Known*, published 80 years after Johnson's death in 1784. Jay wrote that when Johnson moved to Gough Square, "he was a constant visitor to the Cheshire Cheese, because nothing but a hurricane would have induced him to cross Fleet Street," which he would have had to do to get to another coffeehouse or tavern.

"The Street of Ink" or simply "The Street", as Fleet is often called, boasts a long history of journalists, publishers, printers and booksellers. About 1500, Wynkyn de Worde, a German apprentice of William Caxton, the first English printer, set up his press in Fleet Street. He was buried at St. Bride's Church just off Fleet, where Samuel Pepys was baptized in 1633. St. Bride's is full of plaques commemorating journalists, including one from the Second World War, "In Memory of Our Honored Dead," by the

Overseas Press Club of America. All the national and most provincial newspapers had their offices in or near Fleet Street. Today most of the papers are moving out of the City and the Street's five centuries of journalistic history may be coming to an end.

At the eastern end of Fleet Street, in Ludgate Circus, is a plaque on the wall of a bank to **EDGAR WALLACE**, a journalist who, as a boy, sold papers on that corner from which you can look up Ludgate Hill to St. Paul's Cathedral. Wallace's life was Dickensian and emblematic of the opportunities on the Street. Cared for by a Billingsgate fish porter and his wife, he was the illegitimate son of an actor. He left school at twelve, was a newsboy, a soldier in South Africa, a foreign correspondent for the *Daily Mail*, and wrote a vast number of novels, including *The Man Who Knew* (1919) and several thrillers. His plaque reads,

> Edgar Wallace, reporter. Born London 1875. Died Hollywood 1932. Founder Member of the Company of Newspaper Makers. He knew wealth and poverty, yet had walked with kings & kept his bearing. Of his talents he gave lavishly to authorship—but to Fleet Street he gave his heart.

The romance of Fleet Street and the rest of the City is ebbing in the wake of high-rise office buildings. Pepys and Johnson would be appalled at their size. In 1763, Johnson counseled Boswell, "Sir, if you wish to have a just notion of the magnitude of this city, you must not be satisfied with seeing its great streets and squares, but must survey the innumerable little lanes and courts. It is not in the showy evolutions of buildings, but in the multiplicity of human habitations which are crowded together, that the wonderful immensity of London consists."

Fortunately, many little lanes, courts, churches and the Temple remain. And thanks to its illustrious writers, the old City of London, the original literary village, is firmly fixed in the hearts of every lover of English literature.

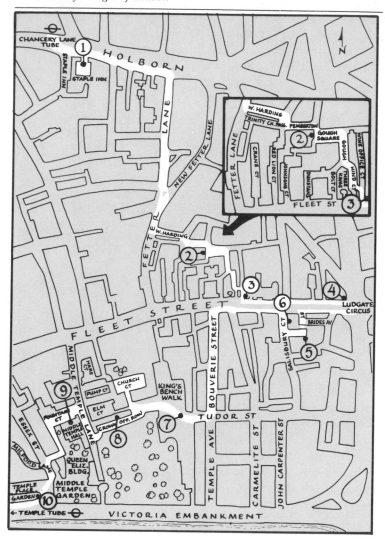

The City

The City Walk

Chancery Lane tube station.

After handing in your ticket in the Chancery Lane tube station, turn right, then go up the left hand staircase to reach the south side of Holborn.

Immediately on your right is the **(1) Staple Inn**, the only medieval building not burned down in the Great Fire of 1666. On your left is the **Dragon Pedestal** marking the entrance to the City of London known as the Square Mile.

Peek into the Staple Inn's court and garden, then walk down Holborn and turn right into Fetter Lane. Cross Fetter Lane at the traffic island at New Fetter Lane, continue a short distance, and turn left into West Harding Street, where there is a sign to Dr. Johnson's house.

Watch for another sign on the right to Pemberton Row and another into Gough Square. The only house in the square was the home of **(2) Dr. Samuel Johnson**.

At the opposite end of Gough Square from Dr. Johnson's house, turn right to the end of the lane, turn left to end of the next lane and right into Wine Office Court where you will find **(3) Ye Old Cheshire Cheese**.

Continue to the end of Wine Office Court into Fleet Street. Turn left to the bottom of the street at Ludgate Circus. On the corner building is a plaque to **(4) Edgar Wallace**.

Cross Fleet Street, turn back up the street and turn left into St. Bride's Avenue leading to **(5) St. Bride's Church** where Samuel Pepys was baptized.

Turn left out of St. Bride's Church, follow the walkway around to the right to St. Bride's Avenue and right again into Salisbury Court to a plaque where **(6) Samuel Pepys** was born.

At the top of Salisbury Court, turn left up Fleet Street, left into

Bouverie Street and right on Tudor Street which leads into **(7)** **The Temple**.

Maps of The Temple grounds and lists of the many authors, including **William Shakespeare** and **Charles Dickens**, and other noted figures associated with the Temple, are in this entrance way and all other archways.

Cross King's Bench Walk into Church Court to see the Temple Church. Return to Crown Office Row where, at No. 2, **(8)** **Charles Lamb** was born.

Continue to Fountain Court past Middle Temple Hall where **(9)** **William Shakespeare**'s *Twelfth Night* was said to have first been performed. Follow the sign to the Queen Elizabeth Building at the left bottom of the court which leads down stairs to Milford Lane and Temple Place.

Cross Temple Place into Victoria Embankment Gardens where there is a statue to **(10) John Stuart Mill**. At the opposite end of the gardens is the Temple tube station.

This walk takes about two hours, longer with a visit to Dr. Johnson's house, a meal, and rests along the walk (or inside St. Bride's Church in inclement weather).

Bloomsbury

> London itself perpetually attracts, stimulates, gives me a play and a
> story and a poem, without any trouble, save that of moving my legs
> through the streets.
>
> — Virginia Woolf, *The Diary*, 1928

"Pish!" said the Lord Mayor of London when the Great Fire of
1666 began, "A woman might pisse it out." Three days later
St. Paul's Cathedral, eighty-six churches and more than thirteen
thousand houses were smoldering ash.

After the Great Fire, Londoners moved to the suburbs. The
squares, designed to be self-contained small villages, were attractive
alternatives to the dangers of crowded city life. Aristocratic
speculators laid out green centers with trees and around them built
rows of fine houses, with less expensive ones behind for servants
and shopkeepers. They planned markets and streets for shops. The
Earl of Southampton, son of Shakespeare's patron, was the
principal landowner and developer in Bloomsbury. His elegant
house stood where Great Russell Street is now, and his gardens
covered the present Southampton Row.

But the most splendid mansion in Bloomsbury was the nearby
Duke of Montagu's. Sad proof that fire can strike anywhere,
Montagu House burned to the ground ten years after the Great
Fire. Less than a century later, in 1754, its rebuilt successor was
bought by public lottery to house the newly established British
Museum.

The museum quickly became a magnet and source of inspiration for writers. John Keats rushed to see the fabled Elgin marbles
and afterward composed "Ode on a Grecian Urn." ISAAC
D'ISRAELI, the prolific author and father of Benjamin Disraeli,
Queen Victoria's beloved Prime Minister, moved close by at 6

Bloomsbury Square in 1818 and was a habitué of the Reading Room.

The American writer, Washington Irving, author of "Rip Van Winkle," described in his *Sketch Book* the old Reading Room of D'Israeli's time (where Irving fell asleep) as being filled with "great cases of venerable books, black-looking portraits of old authors, odd personages, at long tables poring intently over dusty volumes, rummaging among mouldy manuscripts and taking copious notes." According to another contemporary, Isaac D'Israeli was one of those "odd personages," spending "all his life among books . . . either in his own library, or the British Museum Reading Room, or secondhand bookshops of London." But he was not a seedy scholar. D'Israeli was a fine-looking man, noted for his aristocratic features and large, lustrous brown eyes, and he was wealthy enough to indulge his passion for literature.

As an anecdotalist and anthologist, D'Israeli was without rival. Widely read in his day, his six-volume *Curiosities of Literature* began to appear in 1791 and went into twelve editions. He discovered a considerable portion of the letters of Lady Mary Wortley Montagu, that daring traveler and brilliant observer of architecture and exotica in Europe, Turkey and Russia. Because D'Israeli had access to oral traditions and documents now lost, many of his books have been recently republished.

In his Preface to *Curiosities,* D'Israeli asserted, "As authors are scattered through all the ranks of society, among the governors and the governed, . . . we are deeply interested in the secret connection of the incidents of their lives with their intellectual habits." The English public agreed and relished the eccentricities D'Israeli recorded.

"Even great authors have sometimes so much indulged in the seduction of the pen," D'Israeli wrote, "that they appear to have found no substitute for the flow of their ink." He cited the example of Petrarch, the illustrious Italian poet and scholar, who admitted, "I read and I write night and day; it is my only consolation. My eyes are heavy with watching, my hand is weary with writing. On the table where I dine, and by the side of my bed, I have all the materials for writing; and when I awake in the dark, I write, although I am unable to read the next morning what I have written." "Petrarch," D'Israeli observed, "was not always in his perfect senses."

BENJAMIN DISRAELI inherited his father's love of literature. In 1826, when he was twenty-two, he published his first novel, *Vivian Grey.* A decade later he became an MP. Meteoric and demanding as his political life was, it didn't prevent him from writing six more novels. As Prime Minister, he bought the Suez Canal for Queen Victoria, made her Empress of India, and gave her one of his novels. In return, she made him Earl of Beaconsfield and gave him a copy of her *Leaves From A Journal of Our Life in the Highlands.* "Ah, Madame," Disraeli would say to the Queen, "we authors . . ." Isaac D'Israeli would have been proud to know that as his son lay on his deathbed, he was correcting the proofs of his last speech. "I will not," Benjamin Disraeli declared, "go down to posterity talking bad grammar."

During the 1850s, when **CHARLES DICKENS** moved to Tavistock Square, Bloomsbury, the central courtyard of Montagu House was being roofed over with a huge dome to make the new British Museum Reading Room. Dickens was a careful reader. The museum has his letter written to "Geo. Eliot, Esq." after the publication of Eliot's *Scenes of Clerical Life,* saying he suspected the author to be female. But Dickens was not known to be a frequenter of the Reading Room.

For him, the main attraction of Bloomsbury was Tavistock House with an artist's studio that he could convert into a private theater. Dickens was a man of action who loved drama and color; planning the furnishings for and staging private theatricals in his own house afforded him enormous enjoyment. Dickens' mood was such that the streets outside Tavistock House seemed drab.

"The shabbiness of our English capital, as compared with Paris, Bordeaux, Frankfort, Milan, Geneva, almost any important town on the Continent of Europe, . . . I find very striking," he wrote. "The mass of London people are shabby. The absence of distinctive dress has, no doubt, something to do with it. . . As to our women;—next Easter or Whitsuntide look at the bonnets at the British Museum or the National Gallery and think of the pretty white French cap, the Spanish mantilla, or the Genoese mezzero."

Dickens, at this time, was finding married life drab, too. The "bard of domesticity" had fallen in love with another woman, an actress twenty-seven years his junior. Ellen Ternan was eighteen, the same age as his favorite daughter, Kate. She and her sisters had acted in some of the plays Dickens staged, and there were rumors he had eloped to France with her. But he had not.

What he had done was move out of the bedroom at Tavistock House, which he shared with his wife, Catherine, into the dressing room and have the entrance between the two rooms sealed, with a bookcase built against the wall on his side. Catherine, who had borne him ten children, was devastated. As Dickens negotiated a separation from her, he issued position statements to his loyal readers that were printed in the *London Times* and the *New York Herald Tribune*. But not everyone read the story his way. Jane Carlyle's wry observation was that a husband who treated his wife in this manner could, henceforth, be said to have played the dickens with her.

Tavistock House on Tavistock Square was Dickens's final London home and the grandest house that he and Catherine shared. There he wrote *Bleak House, Hard Times, Little Dorrit, A Tale of Two Cities,* and part of *Great Expectations.* "I work slowly and with great care," Dickens said, yet his output was prodigious, even during this period, when his personal life was in turmoil. In 1858, their acrimonious separation final, Catherine moved to Gloucester Crescent and Dickens, although he owned Tavistock House for another two years, left London and moved to Gad's Hill Place, Rochester.

But the inexhaustible vitality of London (as well as Ellen Ternan) kept drawing him back. He knew every quarter of the city—its rookeries and courts, coaching inns and public houses, docks and churches, genteelly shabby homes and the grand houses of nabobs and swells. All his life, Dickens's restless energy sent him looking for more congenial places than London to work, but soon he was back. "The toil and labour of writing day after day without the magic lantern of London is immense," he wrote a friend. "My figures seem to stagnate without crowds around them."

Every Dickens reader visualizes a Victorian London peopled by Dickens. As Tolstoy remarked, "All his characters are my personal friends." Many of Dickens's most memorable characters are immortalized in the names of London thoroughfares such as Pickwick Road, Dorrit Street, Drood Yard, Dombey Street and Copperfield Road.

The Victorian world that Dickens knew was soon to be challenged by a new generation. **GEORGE BERNARD SHAW** was an outrider of the rebellion that began to be associated with Bloomsbury. He was

29 Fitzroy Square, home of G. B. Shaw and, later, Virginia Woolf

sympathetic to Mrs. Dickens's situation under a patriarchal system, and he persuaded her daughter, Kate, not to destroy her mother's correspondence but to donate it to the British Museum. Shaw had come to London as a poor lad from Dublin and educated himself in the British Museum Reading Room. From 1887 to 1898, he lived in poverty and squalor at 29 Fitzroy Square on the edge of Bloomsbury. Then, when he was in his early forties, he was rescued by Charlotte Payne-Townshend, "a green-eyed Irish millionairess," whom he married. Monumentally industrious, Shaw had already achieved fame as an art, music, literature and drama critic. But the plays he wrote at Fitzroy Square, such as *The Philanderer, Mrs Warren's Profession,* and *Arms and the Man,* were considered too shocking to bring him immediately the recognition and wealth he eventually achieved.

When **GERTRUDE STEIN** came to London from America, she did not have to worry about money, as Shaw did. With her brother, Leo, she rented lodgings in Bloomsbury Square. No. 20 was just down the street from the British Museum, where Stein spent her days reading, mostly Elizabethan prose. It was 1902 and she was twenty-nine. Like young people who had flocked to London since Shakespeare's time, she was searching for her *métier.* But London was in no way congenial to Gertrude Stein. She found the streets "infinitely depressing and dismal." Leo fled first, and Gertrude soon followed, to Paris. There she took root, cultivated her inimitable style, and wrote, "To write is to write is to write is to write is to write is to write is to write is to write."

With considerable trepidation, **WILLIAM BUTLER YEATS,** the great Irish poet and later Nobel Prize winner, had plunged into the literary life of London a few years earlier than Gertrude Stein. Like

Shaw, Yeats was a poor Irishman with little education. Both men felt provincial and shy, but Shaw covered his unease with bombast and witticisms, whereas Yeats was painfully aware of his clumsiness and constantly committed social gaffes. He was sure Oscar Wilde disapproved of the color of his shoes.

Yeats often dreamed of retreating back to Ireland. "I bury my head in books," he confessed, "as the ostrich does in the sand."

But in spite of his dreaminess, Yeats quickly became involved in London's literary life. He also became involved with a married woman, and took rooms of his own, in 1895, in Woburn Buildings, Woburn Walk, Bloomsbury. He was thirty and had moved with his parents a few years earlier from Dublin to London. In his own digs, Yeats began work on his first long poem, "The Wanderings of Oisin," which gained him recognition and spurred the Irish literary revival. To complete his new persona, he shaved off his beard and took to wearing black. Yeats was now a true literary dandy, a friend wrote. He wears "the regulation London costume, plus a soft hat, and his ties are dark silk, knotted in a soft bow."

With London as his base, Yeats shuttled between England and Ireland. At Woburn Buildings, he held his famous Monday night "at homes," where poets and writers met. Here Irish nationalists seeking support and encouragement found a sympathetic ear. Yeats was a founder of the Rhymers Club, the Irish Literary Theatre and the influential Abbey Theatre in Dublin. He wrote drama criticism, essays, poems and plays. This intensely productive period of his life, around the turn of the century when he was establishing his reputation, Yeats called his "time of drudgery." Living alone, he worked compulsively, endlessly rewriting and revising his work. At night he could be seen through his window bent over his manuscripts by candlelight.

In his youth, three passions fired Yeats: the occult, Irish nationalism, and love of Maud Gonne. Reputed to be the most beautiful woman in Ireland, Maud Gonne was six feet tall "with the carriage and features of a goddess." She was a fervid nationalist and a fiery orator, and Yeats fell desperately in love with her.

When, in 1903, Maud Gonne rejected him to marry a dashing major, Yeats, who was thirty-seven, felt his world collapse. They agreed to be friends and she remained his inspiration for many years afterwards, but he left London for a lecture tour in the United States.

Back in Bloomsbury, Yeats sought consolation in the spiritualism that had always intrigued him. He went to the seance of an American medium living in Hampstead and she put him in contact with a spirit who announced he was Yeats's guide. The spirit, Leo Africanus, had been an Italian geographer, traveler and poet who had lived among the Moors. The living poet accepted the phantom poet from Fez as his muse. "When I shut my door and light the candle," Yeats wrote, "I invite a Marmorean Muse . . ."

Home of W. B. Yeats in Woburn Walk, Bloomsbury

In 1914 **EZRA POUND**, the American expatriate and poet, appeared at Yeats's door in Woburn Buildings and was soon criticizing his elder's poetry and calling him Uncle William or Old Billyum. The Indian poet, Rabindranath Tagore, came and, like Pound, exercised a great influence on Yeats. Tagore is, Yeats declared, "someone greater than any of us."

Middle age was weighing heavily on Yeats. Friends agreed he needed the stability and companionship of marriage. Then, happily, when he was fifty-two he married Georgie Hyde-Lees, who released his creative energies "like a spring," so that, unlike most poets, he produced his greatest writing in the later period of his life. Being a husband and then a father, Yeats wrote Tagore, made him feel "more knitted into life." He stopped going to seances and in 1919, after twenty-four years, Yeats gave up his bachelor digs in Woburn Walk.

Americans with literary ambitions continued to sail to the source of English literature. When **T. S. ELIOT** arrived in 1914, Ezra Pound took him to meet Yeats at Woburn Walk. But Eliot was bored. The talk of myth and magic left him cold. He turned instead, in the 1920s, to the heart of established Bloomsbury. "If you are back in London," Eliot wrote to **VIRGINIA WOOLF**, ". . . and if and when convenient, I think you might invite me to tea. If so, I shall bring you a new gramophone record."

By this time Virginia and Leonard Woolf were back in Bloomsbury living at Tavistock Square after nine years in Richmond. Poor Tom, as Virginia Woolf called him, had missed the early revolutionary and bohemian period of the Bloomsbury group. Now Virginia and her unique circle of intellectual and gifted friends were influential forces in the literary, artistic and political life of England. They included such famous names as Lytton Strachey, the biographer, Roger Fry and Clive Bell, art critics, and Maynard Keynes, political economist. Virginia was a distinguished critic and novelist. She and Leonard were publishing important new works at their Hogarth Press. In 1922 they published Eliot's *The Waste Land,* the first poem to bring him fame. Eliot worked in Bloomsbury as a director at the firm of Faber & Faber. But he lived in Regent's Park and later in Kensington and Chelsea.

When Virginia, her elder sister Vanessa, and two brothers, Thoby and Adrian, moved in 1904 to 46 Gordon Square, Bloomsbury had become, as Henry James declared, "an antiquated ex-fashionable region." He was appalled that the Stephens children would choose to live there. But it was a deliberate move from the stuffy Victorian home where they had lived with their father until his death. And Bloomsbury had the added attraction of being cheap.

It was at Gordon Square that Thoby, inviting his friends from Cambridge, instituted the regular Thursday evening gatherings that were the genesis of the Bloomsbury group. Virginia and Vanessa had detested the debutante roles they had been forced into. Now on their own, they were free to live the intellectual and artistic lives they craved. Their father, the great Victorian critic and man of letters, Sir Leslie Stephen, had not sent his daughters to school or university, and Virginia, listening to her brother's Cambridge friends, was acutely aware of her own lack of formal education. "Culture for the great majority of educated men's daughters," she later wrote, "must still be that which is acquired outside the sacred gates [of Universities], in public libraries or in private libraries, whose doors by some unaccountable oversight have been left unlocked." To Virginia's delight, the doors to the British Museum Reading Room, just two squares away, were open to her and she went in. In *A Room of One's Own,* Virginia Woolf wrote, "If truth is not to be found on the shelves of the British Museum, where, I asked myself, picking up a notebook and a pencil, is truth?"

Sitting together in Gordon Square, sharing whiskey, coffee and buns, the Bloomsbury group discussed the quest for truth and the meaning of art and life. They challenged Victorian values and conventional wisdom. Virginia began to write perceptive book reviews for *The Times* and other publications. Vanessa, the painter, founded the Friday Club for artists' shoptalk.

Then, in the fall of 1906, Thoby died suddenly. The four Stephen brothers and sisters had taken a holiday abroad, where Thoby contracted typhoid fever. Back home in London, his high fever was misdiagnosed as malaria. The death of their beloved Thoby left a terrible void in Vanessa and Virginia's lives. They struggled to restructure their world.

Vanessa finally agreed to marry Clive Bell, and Adrian and Virginia moved to No. 29 Fitzroy Square, the same house Bernard Shaw had lived in. Now the Bloomsbury group had two houses to

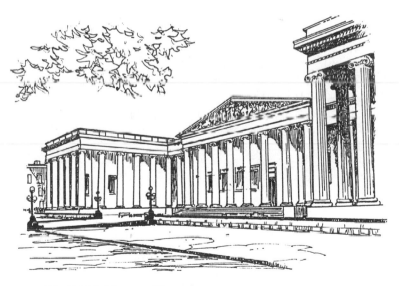

The British Museum, Bloomsbury

meet in, one presided over by Vanessa, the other by Virginia. United by their love of literature and the arts, the two sisters and their brilliant friends continued to rely on each other for social, intellectual and creative stimulus. When Adrian and Virginia moved to a larger house in Bloomsbury on Brunswick Square, they invited economist Maynard Keynes, artist Duncan Grant, and political writer and critic Leonard Woolf to live with them. The following year, 1912, Virginia and Leonard were married, and in 1915, Virginia's first novel, *The Voyage Out,* was published. It received immediate critical acclaim.

The Bloomsbury group enlarged and prospered. They were courted by Lady Ottoline Morrell, an eccentric and generous hostess, who lived at No. 44 Bedford Square. Lady Ottoline had attended Virginia's Thursday evenings in Fitzroy Square and been enchanted by the "long-legged young men" sitting in "basket-chairs smoking pipes and talking . . . of subjects that seemed to me thrilling and exciting. . . . Virginia's bell-like voice would be heard," she recalled, "scattering dull thought" and lighting up "our stagnant prosy minds."

Lady Ottoline's extravagant romanticism was rather cruelly ridiculed by the Bloomsbury group. A tall, forceful woman with a prominent jaw and a penchant for exotic dress, she was, Virginia wrote, "got up to look precisely like the Spanish Armada in full sail." But they accepted her invitations and enjoyed a taste of the grand life that she provided. Among the many non-Bloomsbury writers Lady Ottoline included in her "celebrity salon" were D. H. Lawrence, Katherine Mansfield, Aldous Huxley, Bertrand Russell and William Butler Yeats. She and her husband, Philip Morrell, a Liberal Member of Parliament, bought a country estate, Garsington Manor, near Oxford during World War I. Both Lady Ottoline and Philip were ardent pacifists. They turned Garsington into a haven for conscientious objectors such as Lytton Strachey, who managed to be assigned there as a farm worker during the war.

Then, toward the end of World War I, Lytton Strachey suddenly became a celebrity. His *Eminent Victorians,* published in

1918, was an instant success. Lively, brief, and analytical, it revolutionized the art of biography. It was the first work of "psycho-history," and Strachey was the first of the Bloomsbury writers to attain fame. "I love to hear of Lytton's success," Katherine Mansfield wrote Virginia Woolf. "I put my head out of window at night and expect to find his name pricked upon the heavens in real stars. I feel he is become already a sort of myth, a kind of legend."

Individualistic, energetic and prolific, the Bloomsbury group generated a stream of books, paintings and criticism. Their radical views had sprouted from rebellion and burgeoned to influence and acceptance. In the 1920s they formed a Memoir Club to reminisce and present informal papers of personal recollections. The novelist, **E. M. FORSTER**, an occasional member of Bloomsbury, attended a club meeting and was so moved by memories and his affection for the group that he almost wept. In 1922 Virginia Woolf wrote, "Everyone in Gordon Square has become famous."

Nearly two decades earlier, in the first flush of her independence, Virginia had written to a friend, "We take chairs and sit on our balcony after dinner. . . . Really Gordon Square with the lamps lit and the light on the green is a romantic place." Romance still clings to the squares of Bloomsbury. Spreading copper beech and plane trees shade fragrant, old-fashioned roses blooming along the walks. In the dense greenery birds sing. Of all the great readers and writers who have lived around these secret gardens since the 18th century, it is Virginia Woolf and her luminous circle, in the first quarter of the 20th century, who made Bloomsbury their own.

The Pied Bull, Bloomsbury

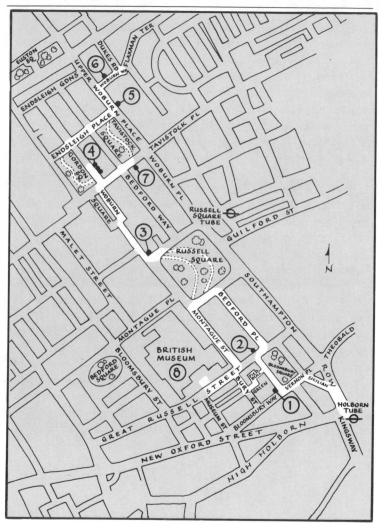

Bloomsbury

Bloomsbury Walk

Holborn tube station.

Cross High Holborn then cross to the left side of Southampton Row.

Walk right one-half block on Southampton Row to the pedestrian arcade, Sicilian Avenue. Go through the arcade to Vernon Place (which becomes Bloomsbury Way).

Jaywalk directly across Vernon Place into Bloomsbury Square and cross the bottom of the square so that you come out facing No. 6 Bloomsbury Square where **(1) Isaac D'Israeli** lived.

Halfway down Bloomsbury Square is a pedestrian entrance into Pied Bull Yard. Detour in to see the restaurants and bookshops but return to Bloomsbury Square and continue to the top of the square where **(2) Gertrude Stein** lived at No. 20.

Walk up Bedford Place to Russell Square. Walk the length of the square coming out the top left corner to No. 24 Russell Square where **(3) T. S. Eliot** worked for the publisher, Faber & Faber.

Take the pedestrian walk to the left of No. 24 Russell Square which leads to Woburn Square. Walk up the right side of Woburn Square to Gordon Square. On the right at Nos. 51, 50 and 46 are blue plaques for **(4) Lytton Strachey**, **Virginia Woolf** and others of the Bloomsbury Group.

Across from No. 46 go through the gate into the square. Walk to the top and come out on Endsleigh Place. Turn right, walk two short blocks and cross Upper Woburn Place. Straight ahead on the British Medical Association Building, BMA House, Tavistock Square, is a plaque for **(5) Charles Dickens** who lived near here in Tavistock House, now demolished.

Turn left, walk a short distance up Upper Woburn Place and right into the pedestrian Woburn Walk where **(6) William Butler Yeats** lived at No. 5. Go to the end of the Walk to see an old building on Flaxman Terrace typical of those in this area when Yeats lived here.

Retrace your steps back to Endsleigh Place. Enter Tavistock Square and walk through to Tavistock Place. No. 52 Tavistock Square where Virginia and Leonard Woolf had their **(7) Hogarth Press** is now gone.

Turn right on Tavistock Place to Woburn Square, left to Russell Square, through the Square, turn right, then left on Montague Street, and right into Great Russell Street to the **(8) British Museum**.

Coming out of the British Museum, turn left on Great Russell Street. At the corner, turn right on Bury Street. A short distance down Bury, turn left into the pedestrian walk, Galen Place.

Turn left at the end of Galen Place and you are back in Pied Bull Court. Come out the covered arcade to Bloomsbury Square, right to Bloomsbury Way, left to Sicilian Avenue, right through the Avenue, another right on Southampton Row and back to the Holborn tube station.

This walk is an easy 1½ to 2 hour stroll, with short rests on the benches in the squares. Include more time for meals or tea in Sicilian Avenue or Woburn Walk and for a visit to the British Museum where there also is a tea room.

Chelsea

> Chelsea is a singular heterogeneous kind of spot, very dirty and confused in some places, quite beautiful in others, abounding in antiquities and traces of great men—Sir Thomas More, Steele, Smollett, etc.
>
> – Thomas Carlyle

FOR MORE THAN two hundred years after that "man for all seasons," Sir Thomas More, moved upriver from the crowded City of London, in about 1525, to a manor house in Chelsea, the village retained its country atmosphere. Scattered houses were surrounded by fields, pastures and orchards. Chelsea's riverside meadows were dotted with buttercups and scored with well-worn footpaths. Roads were few and rough. The smooth, gleaming Thames, thick with thousands of boats, was the grand boulevard of London. Great houses like More's had private stairs down to their gilded barges. At the foot of the public stairs, jams of boatmen in small skiffs cried out for passengers to embark "Eastward Ho!" or "Westward Ho!"

Between the Chelsea Embankment and Battersea Park the Thames retains its regal character, and people in the arts continue to be attracted to Chelsea's stylish riverside ambience. Off the bohemian bustle of King's Road, Chelsea's long, main thoroughfare parallel to the river, many houses where famous literary figures have lived still stand on quiet, narrow, tree-lined streets. Some of those who made their homes in Chelsea were the Scottish couple, Jane and Thomas Carlyle; Americans Mark Twain and Henry James; and the English writers George Eliot, Dante Gabriel Rossetti, Algernon Charles Swinburne and Oscar Wilde.

The house of **SIR THOMAS MORE**, the great humanist and author of *Utopia,* is gone, but his statue stands in the garden close to Chelsea Old Church, where he worshiped. When More lived on the grassy banks of the Thames, King Henry VIII, who delighted in his company, visited him there. But they had a falling out. As the king's Lord Chancellor, More refused to take an oath repudiating papal supremacy. Henry knew that the pope would not declare his marriage to Catherine of Aragon void so that Anne Boleyn could become his legitimate queen. More would not relent in his allegiance to Rome, and the enraged king sent him downriver to the Tower. More was beheaded in 1535.

The martyred Sir Thomas was born in the City on Milk Street in 1478 and educated at St. Anthony's School in Threadneedle Street. Compelled by his father to study law, More entered the Inns of Court. But Latin and Greek literature and theology were closer to his heart than the law. Before he embarked on his brilliant public career as diplomat, Speaker of the House of Commons and Lord Chancellor, More lived for about four years with the monks in the London Charterhouse. There he acquired his life-long habits of austerity. His diet was spare, he slept only five hours a night, spent much time in prayer and meditation and wore a hair shirt. "We must not look at our pleasure to go to heaven in feather beds," he told his daughter, Meg.

But More was a cheerful man. He wrote humorous English verses, and he loved animals. On his grounds in Chelsea he kept an ape, birds, a ferret, a fox, a weasel, and many dogs. Famous in his day for his scholarly writings and for his scathing criticisms of popular superstitions and the religious orders, he is best remembered now for his creative, provocative book, *Utopia.* It is a story full of irony, satire and humorous anecdotes. In it More introduces a mysterious traveler who describes the island, Utopia, which has a perfect social, economic and legal system. "They have no lawyers among them," the traveler declares, "for they consider them as a sort of people whose profession it is to disguise matters." In Utopia both men and women work six hours a day, or less if a surplus is being produced. Before committing themselves to marriage, the bride and groom view each other naked, though both are expected to be virgins. Gold is beaten into chamberpots so that it may not be valued. Cruelty to animals is forbidden. Those who suffer from painful or incurable diseases are advised to commit suicide, but tenderly cared for if they choose not to. Old widowed women are allowed to be priests. Scandalous and original as the attitudes and practices in *Utopia* were, the book established More's reputation as a humanist. *Utopia* was soon translated into most European languages and set the stage for a new literary genre, the Utopian romance.

More was also a pioneer in women's education. He engaged the best scholars to teach his three daughters, who became famous for their learning.

As Sir Thomas was led to the rickety scaffold on Tower Hill, he said, "Assist me up, and in coming down I will shift for myself." His head was impaled on London Bridge. It may have later been thrown in the Thames, or it may have been purchased by More's beloved daughter, Meg, and buried with her in Chelsea Church.

Between Sir Thomas More's beheading in 1535 and the public opening of Ranelagh Gardens in 1742, Chelsea grew as a fashionable area where the wealthy built their houses. Ranelagh was a popular amusement garden built on land abutting the Thames which had belonged to the rich Lord Ranelagh and now belongs to Chelsea Royal Hospital. Lydia in **TOBIAS SMOLLETT**'s novel, *Humphry Clinker*, describes Ranelagh Gardens as an "enchanted palace . . . enlightened with a thousand golden lamps . . . crowded with the great, the rich, the gay, the happy, and the fair." There was dancing in the rotunda, and on the river bank, concerts and genteel walks.

Smollett, an irascible and scatological storyteller, was a Scot unable to eke out a living as a physician. So he turned to writing and in 1751 enjoyed a resounding success with his second novel, *The Adventures of Peregrine Pickle*. Smollett moved to Monmouth House, Chelsea, and like his contemporary, Dr. Samuel Johnson, worked prodigiously, frequented taverns and contracted with booksellers for "standard" works such as a *History of England* and a seven-volume compendium of *Voyages*. Humphry Clinker and Peregrine Pickle, like their creator, are restless characters who delight in travel. Humphry visits Scotland and various parts of England. Peregrine goes to Paris and the Low Countries. And Smollett, at his best as his own protagonist, describes his *Travels Through France and Italy*.

No greater contrast can be imagined than that between popular storyteller Smollett with his great zest for life and travel, and **THOMAS CARLYLE**, a fellow Scot who moved to Chelsea in 1834. Carlyle, the "Sage of Chelsea," was a dour social critic and serious writer avidly read and revered by the Victorian public. Artists and intellectuals came to call but Carlyle seldom budged from Cheyne Row. All the diversion he could handle he found in his tempestuous marriage to the gifted, strong-willed and somewhat spoiled **JANE BAILLIE WELSH**. After her death, in deep remorse for his ill temper and all that she had had to endure, Thomas published Jane's letters, which attest to her brilliance.

Jane and Thomas Carlyle came empty-pocketed to London. Thomas was used to poverty, but Jane had been raised in a well-to-do household, adored and indulged by her father. Early in life she had protested, "I want to learn Latin; please let me be a boy." Her father found her a tutor, and Jane determined to become that Victorian rarity, an educated woman. Thomas recognized Jane's talent and directed her reading. When she complained, "I can feel but I cannot write," he encouraged her with sound advice. Slowly, through a long correspondence, she became his pupil. Eventually she consented to marry him.

Although Thomas nurtured Jane's ambition to write, he saw himself as the writer in the family. "Do you not think," he asked Jane, "that when you on one side of our household shall have faithfully gone thro your housewife duties, and I on the other shall have written my allotted pages, we meet over our frugal meal with far happier and prouder hearts than thousands who are not blessed with any duties?"

No. 5 (now 24) Cheyne Row, where the Carlyles lived for nearly fifty years, was more a battlefield than a dwelling place, observed Virginia Woolf a century later after visiting the tall brick house. It must have been "full of books and coal smoke," she wrote, with Jane fighting an "incessant battle" against cold and dirt and bugs in the woodwork. The water pump was in the kitchen basement and coal had to be carried to fireplaces in each room. "Both husband and wife had genius; they loved each other; but what," Woolf wondered, "can genius and love avail against bugs and tin baths and pumps in the basement?"

Thomas at least was delighted to find the house. He wrote describing it to Jane as in "a genteel neighborhood . . . The house itself is eminent, antique" with "floors thick as a rock, wood of them here and there worm-eaten, yet capable of cleanness." Cheyne Row, he said, "runs out upon a Parade . . . along the shore of the river, a broad highway with huge shady trees . . . the broad river with white-trowsered, white-shirted Cockneys dashing by like arrows in their long canoes of boats."

According to Carlyle, Chelsea was "a singular heterogeneous kind of spot, very dirty and confused in some places, quite beautiful in others, abounding in antiquities and traces of great men." He went walking "along Battersea Bridge and thence by a wondrous path across cornfields, mud ditches, river embankments," and watched "steamers snorting about the river, each with a lantern at its nose." But the neighborhood became noisier. Crowing roosters, organ grinders, street hawkers and horses' hooves clattering down the cobblestone streets distracted Thomas from his writing. In desperation he had the top floor of the house insulated with double walls and provided with a skylight instead of windows to make a "sound-proof" study. But it proved to be "the noisiest room in the house," too cold in winter, too hot in summer. Irritably, Carlyle migrated back downstairs to the dining room table. "A well-written life," declared the great biographer, "is almost as rare as a well-spent one."

An insomniac and dyspeptic, Thomas Carlyle was a trial to himself and to Jane. "If peace and quiet be not in one's own power," she wrote, "one can always give oneself at least bodily fatigue—no such bad *succe daneum* after all." Caring for the house and her famous husband provided Jane with fatigue in full measure. But her lively mind and quick wit gained her admirers in her own right.

Carlyle dubbed economics "the Dismal Science," gave us the phrase, my "house my castle is," and wrote, "No man who has once heartily and wholly laughed can be altogether irreclaimably bad."

Thomas Carlyle, Chelsea

When **JOHN STUART MILL**, the great economist, gave Carlyle the dreadful news that the whole manuscript of his first volume of his history of the French Revolution, which Mill had borrowed, had been used by his maid to start a fire, Carlyle had reason to be angry. He had not kept a draft of his final text and he had destroyed his notes. And he and Jane were still bitterly poor. But when he recovered from his shock, Thomas said to Jane, "Mill, poor fellow, is terribly cut up; we must endeavour to hide from him how serious this business is to us."

Carlyle immediately set to work and in five months rewrote the complete volume. *The French Revolution* published in three volumes in 1837 made him famous.

When **GEORGE ELIOT** moved into her beautiful house overlooking the Thames on Cheyne Walk in 1880, just a year before Thomas Carlyle died, she already was a famous novelist. *Adam Bede, Mill on the Floss,* and *Silas Marner* had established her reputation, and *Middlemarch* was acclaimed as one of the greatest novels of the century. As a young woman, Mary Ann Evans had worked as a writer, translator and editor, joined a group of intellectuals that included Alfred Tennyson and Charles Dickens, and adopted the pen name of George Eliot to conceal her sex. When she was thirty-three years old she entered into a relationship with George Henry Lewes, a married man who was separated from his wife but unable to obtain a divorce. Lewes helped George Eliot realize her literary gifts. She called herself Mrs. Lewes and intimate friends accepted them as a married couple but the liaison was considered scandalous in Victorian society. Yet it was a happy, productive relationship that lasted nearly a quarter of a century until Lewes died in 1878.

Alone, George Eliot was miserable. Then, to her friends' shock and surprise, in her sixty-first year, she married a vigorous, handsome man of forty, John Cross, an American banker in London, who had been a friend of both hers and Lewes's.

"Marriage has seemed to restore my old self," George Eliot wrote. "I was getting hard, and if I had decided differently I think I should have become very selfish."

John and Mary Ann went to Venice for their honeymoon. Five months after their marriage the Crosses settled into their townhouse at No.4 Cheyne Walk. "I indulge the hope," Mary Ann wrote a friend, "that you will some day look at the river from the windows of our Chelsea house, which is rather quaint and picturesque."

On December 18, 1880, about two weeks after they had moved in, John and Mary Ann went to a concert at St. James's Hall. She caught a chill and awoke next morning with a sore throat. Three days later Mary Ann Evans was dead. As George Eliot, the great novelist, she had hoped to be buried in Westminster Abbey. But even her literary friends would not countenance a freethinking woman's receiving such an honor. Not until a hundred years later was a memorial stone with both her names, Mary Ann Evans and George Eliot, installed in the Poets' Corner.

The irregularities of George Eliot's Victorian neighbors on Cheyne Walk were of a different sort from hers. A few houses down, at No. 15, poet and painter **DANTE GABRIEL ROSSETTI** kept a menagerie in his garden. The rabbits, marmot, raccoon, deer, wombat and kangaroo were not as disturbing as the braying jackass and shrieking peacocks, which became the bane of the neighborhood. The armadillos caused havoc by burrowing out of Rossetti's garden and, once, into a next-door basement.

Rossetti moved to Cheyne Walk after the death of his wife in 1862, and for twenty years until his own death his house was the center of bohemian life in London. **ALGERNON CHARLES SWINBURNE,** a poet with flaming red hair and bulging forehead, was the *enfant terrible* of Rossetti's pre-Raphaelite group. For a while Swinburne lived at No.15. Rossetti's house, filled with bizarre furniture, enormous statuary and exotic animals, was a showcase for its wayward and merry inhabitant. In order to renew the lease he finally had to agree to a clause that has become a standard item for Chelsea landlords: tenants are not allowed to keep peacocks in their gardens.

After Rossetti, **OSCAR WILDE** became the leader of the avant-guarde art world and was the rage of London until his sensational trial and conviction for homosexual practices brought his downfall. The "magician of Chelsea" was born in Dublin. He gained a reputation for his brilliant wit at Oxford, won a prestigious poetry prize and came to London as a minor celebrity. A speaking tour of the United States in 1882 increased his following, and his witticisms continue to be quoted. "I never travel without my diary," he wrote. "One should always have something sensational to read in the train."

Wilde was wicked. He declared art the only reason for life, lived like a dandy, poked fun at pomposity and observed acutely, "The youth of America is their oldest tradition. It has been going on now for three hundred years."

The money Constance Mary Lloyd brought to their marriage Wilde used to decorate their Tite Street house in "Good Taste"— the subject of one of his popular lectures. In the drawing room the ceiling designed by James Whistler had two real peacock feathers in it, and the dining room was done entirely in different shades of white. The walls of his bedroom were red and gold. In his downstairs study, which looked out on the street, the walls were painted buttercup yellow, the woodwork lacquered red; in the corner on a red stand was a cast of the Hermes of Praxiteles. To inspire him, Wilde worked at a table that had belonged to plain and frugal Thomas Carlyle.

Magazines were full of pictures and descriptions of Wilde's Chelsea house. His novel, *The Picture of Dorian Gray*, and his plays, including *Lady Windermere's Fan* and his masterpiece, *The Importance of Being Earnest* (perennial favorites in England) were enormous successes. Then, at the height of his career, Wilde sued the marquess of Queensberry, father of his friend Lord Alfred Douglas, for libel. Wilde lost and was sentenced to two years of hard labor in Reading Gaol. He could have fled to the Continent; instead he sat drinking hock and seltzer with Lord Alfred at the Cadogan Hotel on Sloane Street waiting to be arrested.

The scandal of Wilde's homosexual affairs and his conviction filled the newspapers in England, Europe and America. Initially his friends feared defending him, but eventually people of goodwill spoke out for his right to a private life. Mrs. Patrick Campbell, the famous actress, made the memorable remark, "I don't care what they do as long as they don't do it in the street and frighten the horses."

HENRY JAMES was sickened by the whole affair. "He Wilde was never in the smallest degree interesting to me—but this hideous human history has made him so—in a manner." The great novelist, author of *Daisy Miller, The Bostonians* and *The Turn of the Screw,* was interested in psychological subtleties and motivations. In his books he posed "raw America against refined Europe." James found England a more congenial place to work than his native New York and Boston, and he lived at a number of London addresses. During the last few years of his life, until his death in 1916, he kept a flat around the corner from the Carlyles' house at Carlyle Mansions, 21 Cheyne Walk, with a magnificent view of the river. T. S. Eliot's rooms were directly below. "The Embankment, which is admirable, if not particularly interesting, does what it can," wrote James, "and the mannered houses of Chelsea stare across at Battersea Park like eighteenth-century ladies surveying a horrid wilderness."

Another American author attracted to Chelsea was **MARK TWAIN**, although his sojourn at Tedworth Square was brief—from 1896 to 1898—and uncharacteristically secluded. The internationally famous humorist stopped in London at the conclusion of a world lecture tour, or "lecture raid" as he called it, which he had undertaken to pay off massive debts from a business failure. There he received the tragic news that his favorite daughter, Suzy, had died. Mark Twain was plunged into grief. He shunned society and began a writing regime for a travel book called *Following the Equator*. Each day he took his customary hour's walk down King's Road observing "Shakespeare people." After a reporter called at his red brick house in quiet Tedworth Square to see if he were still alive, Mark Twain cabled the Associated Press in New York, "The reports of my death are greatly exaggerated."

Passenger boat service on the Thames from Chelsea to the City is showing signs of life, too. Though river travel will never be as colorful or crowded as it was in Sir Thomas More's day, residents now can commute in catamarans powered by water-jet from Chelsea Harbour to West India Docks. As they jet upriver in the dusk after a long day at the office, commuters may recall a scene from the film, *A Man For All Seasons*. It was a dark night. Sir Thomas More emerged from a trying session with Henry VIII at Hampton Court. He was drained and wanted to be rowed quickly back home to Chelsea. But the boatmen knew the Lord Chancellor had incurred the king's wrath. As a signal of their refusal to row the doomed Sir Thomas, one by one they plunged their lighted torches into the black waters of the Thames.

Chelsea's literary history is dense with drama. King's Road is a continual carnival. And down the village side streets one may imagine a host of Chelsean writers walking out to take the air along the Embankment.

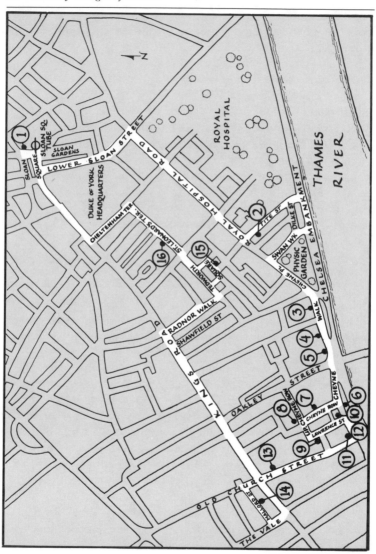

Chelsea

Chelsea Walk

Sloane Square tube station

On your right out of the tube station is **(1) Royal Court Theatre**, home of plays by **George Bernard Shaw, John Osborne** and other controversial playwrights.

Cross Sloane Gardens straight ahead from the tube station, turn left into Lower Sloane Street, right on Royal Hospital Road, past Sir Christopher Wren's Royal Hospital, and left on Tite Street where **(2) Oscar Wilde** lived at No. 34.

Continue on Tite Street to Chelsea Embankment, right on Swan Walk past the Physic Garden, left on Cheyne Place which angles right into Cheyne Walk. **(3) George Eliot** lived at No. 4 Cheyne Walk, **(4) Dante Gabriel Rossetti** and **Algernon Charles Swinburne** at No. 16 (Tudor House) and **(5) Henry James** at No. 21.

Continue on Cheyne Walk, cross Oakley Street (do not follow sign to Carlyle's house) into small park with statue of **(6) Thomas Carlyle**. Turn right at the statue into Cheyne Row where at No. 5 is the home of **(7) Jane** and **Thomas Carlyle**.

Turn right out of the Carlyle house to Upper Cheyne Row where on the right at No. 22 is the home of **(8) Leigh Hunt**. Turn left on Lawrence Street where No. 16 was the home of **(9) Tobias Smollett**.

At the corner of Lawrence Street and Cheyne Walk is Carlyle Mansions where **(10) Henry James** and **T. S. Eliot** lived. Turn right into the courtyard of Chelsea Old Church where there is a statue of **(11) Sir Thomas More**. Inside the church is a plaque commemorating **(12) Henry James**.

Go right on Old Church Street to St. Luke's Rectory, No. 56, the boyhood home of **(13) Charles Kingsley**. Cross King's Road, staying on Old Church Street, then left on Mallord Street to No. 13, home of **(14) A. A. Milne** and birthplace of Winnie the Pooh.

At the end of Mallord Street, turn left into The Vale, then left on King's Road to Radnor Walk. (Note Shawfield Street, the street before Radnor Walk, whose sign is behind you and hard to see as you come up King's Row.) Go right on Radnor Walk to Tedworth Square.

Walk around Tedworth Square to No.23, home of **(15) Mark Twain**.

Right on St. Leonard Terrace to No.18, home of **(16) Bram Stoker**. Left on Cheltenham Terrace, right into King's Road to the Sloan Square tube station.

This is a rather longer, approximately 2 to 2½ hour walk not including a visit to Carlyle's house, meals, poking into shops on King's Road and resting on one of the many benches in the parks and on the streets.

The Chelsea Embankment

Hampstead

I met Wordsworth on Hampstead Heath this morning . . .
– John Keats

THE HILLSIDE VILLAGE of Hampstead has attracted writers from Dr. Samuel Johnson in the eighteenth century to that modern master of spy novels, JOHN LE CARRÉ. One of the great attractions of Hampstead is the eight hundred acres of open heath and forest that edge the village. Dedicated walkers on Hampstead Heath, like Le Carré, quit their desks to stride across meadows, around ponds, and into deep vine-tangled woods. Even DR. JOHNSON, who was not a man to leave his beloved City, wrote during his brief stay in Hampstead in 1748, "The needy traveller, serene and gay, / Walks the wild heath, and sings his toils away."

Johnson had come to Hampstead to visit his wife, Tetty, who was hoping to regain her health there. By the eighteenth century, Hampstead had become a fashionable village noted for its medicinal waters and clear air. Hampstead Heath, the highest point and largest open space in London, guaranteed fresh unpolluted air. Drinking Hampstead's spring water which is impregnated with iron salts, was alleged to cure most ailments. In the Vale of Health, near the pond at the edge of Hampstead Heath, long tables were set up where tea was served for a few pence, and later on a hotel was built. In the nineteenth century, Jack Straw's Castle, above the Vale of Health, was a favorite inn of many writers, among them Dickens, who invited a friend to join him there for a chop and glass of red wine: "You don't feel disposed, do you, to muffle yourself up, and start off with me for a good brisk walk over Hampstead-heath?"

Hampstead's reputation is intellectual and arty. Only four miles from the center of the City of London, it is now an integral part of Greater London. But Hampstead is still a world away in atmosphere. Its architecture is a charming jumble of Georgian, Victorian and Edwardian mansions and terraced cottages, red brick and white stucco, graced with ivy and roses, wisteria and holly. Its steep streets and sudden views make some residents feel as if they live on a mountain. From Parliament Hill at the top of Hampstead Heath is a sweeping view down to the spires and concrete office blocks of London.

The village of Hampstead was first mentioned in William the Conqueror's great survey of England, the Domesday Book of 1086. That record shows that the Abbot of St. Peter owned Hampstead, the villagers owned one plow and there were one hundred pigs in the woodland.

Today the crisscrossed pathways, maze of narrow streets, stepped lanes and alleyways render Hampstead a map-maker's nightmare. Tucked away down a footpath in the Vale of Health is a cottage much like the one **LEIGH HUNT** lived in on this site from 1816 until 1821. Hunt, a poet, essayist and editor, printed in his newspaper John Keats' first poem, "O Solitude." He was the center of a literary circle and a great friend of that triumvirate of English romantic poets, Byron, Shelley and Keats. His home was always open to them. Keats often slept on a sofa in Hunt's library. Shelley came and sailed paper boats on the heath ponds nearby. And when Shelley and Byron traveled to Italy, Hunt went with them.

He also went to prison for libeling the Prince Regent. In his radical newspaper, *The Examiner*, Leigh Hunt called the prince a fat Adonis of fifty and "a violator of his word, a libertine over head and ears in disgrace." He was sentenced to two years.

In his poem, "Written after Hunt's Release from Jail," (similar in title to Keats's "Written on the Day that Mr. Leigh Hunt left

Prison") Hunt expressed his love of walking on the heath:

> And cottaged vales with billowy fields beyond,
>   And clump of darkening pines, and prospects blue,
> And that clear path through all, where daily meet
>   Cool cheeks, and brilliant eyes, and morn-elastic feet.

Before moving to Hampstead, Leigh Hunt, his wife and seven children lived at Upper Cheyne Row around the corner from Jane and Thomas Carlyle in Chelsea. Thomas thoroughly disapproved of the way the Hunts and their "whole school of well-conditioned wild children" lived. He saw Hunt's house as a "political Tinkerdom" full of "hucksters," while all over "the dusty table and ragged carpet lie all kinds of litter—books, papers, egg-shells, scissors," and the torn out heart of a loaf of bread. **JANE** (or **JENNY) CARLYLE,** the consummate thrifty housewife, often was exasperated with the Hunts' slovenly improvidence, but she had a soft spot for them. When Leigh was ill during an influenza epidemic she anxiously inquired after him. As soon as he recovered, Hunt, touched by her solicitude, surprised Jenny with a visit. Startled, she jumped up and kissed him, thus inspiring Hunt to write,

> Say I'm weary, say I'm sad,
>   Say that health and wealth have missed me,
> Say I'm growing old, but add,
>   Jenny kissed me.

JOHN KEATS was studying medicine when he met Leigh Hunt, who introduced him to the London world of young artists and writers. A fellow medical student had called Keats "an idle loafing fellow, always writing poetry." But Keats had qualified as a licentiate of the Society of Apothecaries, been apprenticed to a surgeon and made his hospital rounds cleaning wounds and setting bones. It was after he joined Hunt's literary circle that he made a firm commitment to poetry. "I am convinced more and more, day by day," he wrote, "that fine writing is, next to fine doing, the top thing in the world."

The next year, 1817, John Keats moved to Well Walk, Hampstead, with his brother Tom, whom he nursed until Tom's death from tuberculosis in December 1818. Keats's friend, Charles Brown, then asked him to share his house in Hampstead. Brown and another friend of Keats, Charles Wentworth Dilke, had built a double villa well back from the road in a large garden. Each of the men occupied half of the house, now called Wentworth Place, which was divided by a stout wall. Brown rented Keats a small sitting room with a bedroom above at the back of his side of the house and charged him five pounds a month for his board and lodging.

When Dilke moved out in 1819, Mrs. Brawne and her three children moved into his half of the house. John Keats promptly fell in love with Mrs. Brawne's daughter, Fanny, who was eighteen. Fanny, Keats wrote his brother, George, "is beautiful and elegant, graceful, silly, fashionable and strange—we have a little tiff now and then." Keats passionately poured out his love in letters to Fanny and they became engaged. "I almost wish we were butterflies and liv'd but three summer days," he wrote. "—three such days with you I could fill with more delight than 50 common years could ever contain."

But theirs was a doomed passion. Keats had less than three years to live. Already he was ill with tuberculosis. Yet in the short time that he had, Keats produced an astonishing body of work. At Wentworth Place, faithfully tended by his friends and Fanny and her mother, he wrote his finest poetry including his great odes, "On a Grecian Urn," "To Psyche," "To Autumn" and others.

Brown recalled how Keats was inspired by the song of a nightingale that had built its nest in a tree in the garden: "Keats felt a tranquil and continual joy in her song, and one morning he took his chair from the breakfast-table to the grass-plot under a plum-tree where he sat for two or three hours. When he came into the house," Brown wrote, "I perceived he had some scraps of paper

in his hand, and these he was quietly thrusting behind the books."
On those scraps Keats had written his much loved "Ode to a
Nightingale."

"A thing of beauty is a joy forever," Keats declared in
Endymion. In "Ode on a Grecian Urn," he went further to say,
"Beauty is truth, truth beauty'—that is all / Ye know on earth, and
all ye need to know." Critics still quarrel over the meaning of this
well-known couplet and some have concluded that it is ambiguous
and a poor ending to a superb poem.

"Only one presence—that of Keats himself—dwells here,"
Virginia Woolf observed when she visited Wentworth Place in the
1930s. But, she thought, the impression Keats left was "not of
fever, but of that clarity and dignity which come from order and
self-control." Even as he grew weaker, Keats continued to work.
"Whenever I find myself growing vaporish," he wrote, "I rouse
myself, wash and put on a clean shirt, brush my hair and clothes,

The Keats house (Wentworth Place), Hampstead

tie my shoestrings neatly, and in fact adonize as if I were going out—then, all clean and comfortable I sit down to write."

Walking on the heath, Keats met not only Wordsworth, but Coleridge, who remembered that after they were introduced and parted, Keats turned back to say, "Let me carry away the memory, Coleridge, of having pressed your hand." As Coleridge shook the young man's hand, the older poet recalled thinking, "There was death in that hand."

Keats knew he was dying. Climbing between the cold sheets in his little bedroom after catching a chill on the coach from London, he coughed up blood. "Bring me the candle, Brown," he said. As his faithful friend recorded, Keats "looked up in my face, with a calmness of countenance that I can never forget, and said: "I know the colour of that blood;—it is arterial blood;—I cannot be deceived in that colour; that drop of blood is my death-warrant—I must die." A year later, on February 23, 1821, when he was twenty-six years old, John Keats died in Rome.

In 1894 a group of American admirers of Keats erected a marble bust of him in Hampstead Parish Church, and in the 1920s American poet Amy Lowell and her Boston Committee raised half the purchase price of Wentworth Place as a memorial to John Keats.

ROBERT LOUIS STEVENSON, like Keats, suffered from tuberculosis. Because his father insisted, he was studying law, but he yearned to write and had, since he was a teenager, set himself to learn the writer's craft. After a severe bout of illness when he was twenty-three, the doctor ordered him out of his native Scotland to a warmer climate in the south of France. The next year, 1874, Stevenson stayed at Abernethy House on Mount Vernon up Holly Walk from Hampstead Parish Church. "Hampstead is the most delightful place for air and scenery," he wrote a friend in Scotland. "I cannot understand how the air is so good."

Stevenson went "walking and strolling about the heath," and wrote furiously. "Youth," he later noted, "is wholly experimental." That year his essay, "Ordered South," appeared in *Macmillan's* magazine and another in *Cornhill,* then edited by Leslie Stephen, father of Virginia Woolf. The following year Stevenson was called to the Scottish bar, but he never practiced. Unlike that of Keats, Stevenson's writing career developed slowly, but he had longer to live. For the rest of his life, until he died in the South Seas at the age of forty-four, the author of *Treasure Island, Kidnapped* and *A Child's Garden of Verses* traveled in search of health.

A villa in Hampstead was a refuge for **RABINDRANATH TAGORE,** the great Indian poet, when he visited London in 1912. He was suffering from cultural shock. He had left his native India, where the climate is hot and life is carried on outdoors, in public, and where one is constantly surrounded by family and friends. In a London hotel he was in despair. The English climate was cold and people hurried inside, guarding their privacy behind closed doors. "Everyone seemed like phantoms," he noted. "The hotel used to empty after breakfast and I watched the crowded streets. . . . It was not possible to know this humanity or enter into the heart of another place." But an Englishman, William Rothenstein, who admired the translation from Bengali of Tagore's *The Songs of Gitanjali,* befriended him and found him more congenial lodgings at No.3, Villas on the Heath, Vale of Health in Hampstead. A year later, Tagore won the Nobel Prize for Literature and in 1915 was awarded a knighthood.

D. H. LAWRENCE's brief stay in Hampstead in 1915 ended far less happily than Tagore's. He, too, lived in the Vale of Health. "You come to Hampstead tube station," he directed Lady Cynthia ground floor at No.1 of a row of rather ugly, bow-front brick houses. The peripatetic, impoverished Lawrences were to live briefly at a number of addresses in Hampstead. "We are struggling on with the furnishing," Lawrence moaned. "The infinite is now swallowed up in chairs and scrubbing brushes and wastepaper baskets, as far as I am concerned."

Three years earlier, Lawrence had called on Professor Ernest Weekley in Well Walk, Hampstead, about a teaching post. A month later he eloped with the professor's wife, Frieda, daughter of the German aristocrat Baron Friedrich von Richthofen. The period in the Vale of Health was a particularly miserable time in his and Frieda's tempestuous lives. World War I was raging, and Lawrence was raging against it and against the new industrial technologies and the loss of old simplicities. Because he was tubercular, Lawrence was exempt from military service. He and Frieda were walking on Hampstead Heath on September 8 when they saw the first zeppelin attack on London. The zeppelin was "just above us," Lawrence reported, "quite small, among a fragile incandescence of clouds. And underneath it were splashes of fire as the shells from earth burst. . . . It seemed as if the cosmic order were gone, as if there had come a new order . . . So it is the end—our world is gone, and we are like dust in the air."

Lawrence had had many dreams of better ways to live, including communities of like-minded people, beginning with his friends, Katherine Mansfield and her husband, John Middleton Murry. But in 1915, Lawrence's novel, *The Rainbow,* was officially declared obscene and ordered suppressed. It was, Lawrence felt, "the end of my writing in England." Authorities were hounding him because of Frieda's German origin, and the embittered Lawrences decided to leave the country. In December 1915, Lawrence wrote, "The flat in the Vale of Health is empty, the Asquith, "walk up the hill and along past the pond to Jack Straw's Castle, drop down the Heath on the path opposite the inn, at the bottom swerve round to the right into the Vale, and there is Byron Villas before your eyes." Lawrence and his wife, Frieda, lived on the furniture sold or given away, the lease transferred to another man. We go back there no more." The author of *Sons and Lovers* and *Women in Love* finally reached Taos, New Mexico, by way of Italy six years later. "The novel is the highest example of subtle interrelatedness that man has discovered," he declared. It can "make the whole man tremble."

A deep friendship existed between D. H. Lawrence and **KATHERINE MANSFIELD**, one of the pioneers of the modern short story. Both were extraordinarily gifted imaginative writers. They admired and understood each other, and Lawrence incorporated attributes of Mansfield's character and appearance into several of his fictitious characters. Mansfield recognized the brilliance of his work even though she intensely disliked some of his seamy scenes and sexual descriptions. Eventually they quarreled, Lawrence threw one of his "spectacular rages," and they remained estranged for many years. Each, however, harbored a sufficiently deep affection and respect for the other to enable a kind of a reconciliation to be effected near the end of Katherine's life.

When Mansfield, who was born in New Zealand, married the English literary journalist, John Middleton Murry, in 1918, they agreed, Murry wrote, "that I should look for a house in Hampstead, and I found a tall grey brick one, outwardly unprepossessing, but immediately overlooking the Heath. Because of its greyness and its size we christened it the Elephant." Mansfield liked the views and the way the sunlight flooded in through the tall windows. Even though she was already seriously ill with tuberculosis, she delighted in fixing up the house. "All the doors are to be grey, and the skirting boards, &c and shutters," she wrote a friend, "with black stair banisters and black treads. In the kitchen, white distemper with turquoise blue paint. On the top floor your room—lemon yellow with grey cupboard. The bathroom real canary yellow—and the external paint for the railings, gate and door, grey again."

During the periods when Mansfield was well enough to enjoy life, she and Murry gave a few parties, she saw friends, took short walks on the heath, treated her cats to cream from a silver spoon and lay in bed reading poetry with Murry.

One of Mansfield's visitors at East Heath Road was Virginia Woolf. The two were both rivals and friends. Woolf describes in her journal how edgy at first they were with each other, but then how they "fell into step" and talked easily and long about "our precious art." Although Katherine favored a far more bohemian life than Virginia, the two had much in common: both were fiercely and foremost dedicated to their writing. "Looking back," Katherine Mansfield notes, "I imagine I was always writing." Yet their friendship never fully developed. Virginia remembered one of her last visits to the house in Hampstead: "I go up. She Katherine gets up very slowly from her writing table. A glass of milk & a medicine bottle stood there. There were also piles of novels. Everything was very tidy, bright & somehow like a dolls house." Katherine "half lay on the sofa by the window. She had her look of a Japanese doll, with the fringe combed quite straight across her head."

Katherine Mansfield left Hampstead in 1920 for France in a desperate search for a cure. "Whenever I prepare for a journey I prepare as though for death," she noted in her journal. "Should I never return, all is in order. This is what life has taught me." She never returned to the tall grey house on East Heath Road in Hampstead. Death claimed the still growing but already recognized author of such brilliant stories as "The Garden Party," "At the Bay," and "The Daughters of the Late Colonel," just a few months after she turned thirty-five.

Set behind a low wall on Admiral's Walk is Grove Lodge, in white stucco with dark shutters and boxes of red geraniums, where the chronicler of the Forsyte family, **JOHN GALSWORTHY**, lived for fifteen years. Galsworthy's story of a wealthy middle-class family over a forty year period was made into a BBC film that became a worldwide hit. The Forsytes were similar to the author's own property-rich family who had attained success in the business and professional worlds. But none of the fictional Forsytes lived in Hampstead. Irene in The *Forsyte Saga* was modeled, to some extent, on Ada Galsworthy, the wife of Galsworthy's cousin, with whom the novelist carried on a secret affair for ten years. Ada first encouraged Galsworthy, who like so many writers before him found his legal profession uncongenial, to write. He first published under a pseudonym but in 1905 married the divorced Ada and the next year published, under his own name, his most famous novel, *A Man of Property*. It is the first novel in the *Saga* and establishes his theme that the desire for property is morally wrong. In 1932 John Galsworthy received the Nobel Prize for Literature, and in 1933 he died at Grove Lodge where, in his study overlooking the garden, he had written most of the *Saga*.

Grove Lodge, John Galsworthy's home in Hampstead

GEORGE ORWELL, author of *Animal Farm* and *1984*, was as interested in politics as Galsworthy was not. Both writers rejected the values of the class they were born and educated to. Galsworthy attended Harrow and Oxford, and Orwell went to Eton. But Galsworthy was independently wealthy while Orwell struggled all of his life to eke out a living. After he returned from serving with the Indian Imperial Police in Burma, Orwell worked part time, during 1934–35, in a bookshop in Hampstead. "Book-lover's Corner" was at the bottom of South End Road in a small shopping area.

As Orwell described it in *Keep the Aspidistra Flying,* the shop "stood on a corner, on a sort of shapeless square where four streets converged. To the left, just within sight of the door, stood a great elm-tree." It was and still is a busy corner noisy with buses and cars and people walking up the hill from the underground. George Orwell lived in a flat above the shop. In the mornings and evenings he wrote and in the afternoons he worked in the bookshop. A sharp observer of class differences, Orwell noted that "there were high brow, middle brow and low brow books, new and second-hand all jostling together, as befitted this intellectual and social borderland."

Orwell attended some of the poetry sessions held in Hampstead and on one occasion took his mother, who, so the story goes, was so bored she slept through most of the reading. Another time he read Keats to the gathering. But Orwell's stay in Hampstead was short. He had a distinct distaste for anything like a bohemian life and a deep distrust of association with any group. Hampstead did not hold him as it did more romantic writers who found their inspiration in this most green and gracious village.

Each literary village imparts a sense of place well loved by the writers who lived there. "How beautiful a London street is," Virginia Woolf wrote. She went out to buy a pencil, noting with pleasure what she saw "rambling the streets of London" on her way to the stationary store. She passed second-hand bookstores and skirted tree-filled squares with iron railings where "one hears those little cracklings and stirrings of leaf and twig." Glancing at the windows of offices she imagined "fierce lights burn over maps, over documents, over desks where clerks sit turning with wetted forefinger the files of endless correspondence." And in her mind's eye she filled a house with easy chairs, papers, china, perhaps an inlaid table and a woman "measuring out the precise number of spoons for tea."

It is "the wonderful immensity of London," as Dr. Johnson said, that has inspired writers from Chaucer to Shakespeare, Pepys, Keats, Carlyle and Woolf. Writers have enriched our visions of the villages where they lived so that when we walk down the streets of the City or Bloomsbury, Chelsea or Hampstead, we can see more than meets the eye: the young Shakespeare in stockings and doublet hurrying across the garden of the Inns of Court; the portly figure of Dr. Johnson, book in hand, entering the Cheshire Cheese; Keats on a sunny day sitting in the shade of a plum tree listening to a nightingale sing; tall, bearded Carlyle striding purposefully along the Chelsea embankment; Yeats bent over his desk by the window in Woburn Walk; and Virginia Woolf taking her chair out on the balcony to sit beside her sister, Vanessa, at 46 Gordon Square.

What Isaac D'Israeli called "the delights of reading" enhance the eye of the beholder. So take your book, find a bench and let these literary villages become your own.

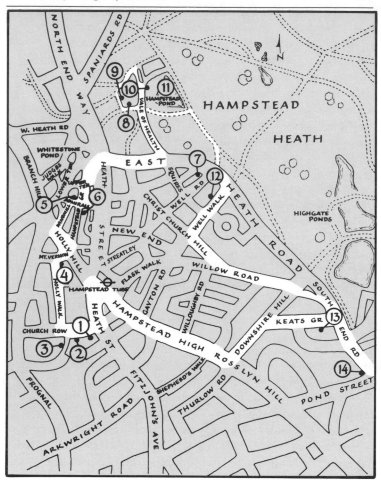

Hampstead

Hampstead Walk

Hampstead tube station

Walk down Heath Street and turn right into Church Row. No. 27 is where **(1) Daphne du Maurier** was born and No. 17 where **(2) Arnold Bennett** lived.

Continue on Church Row to the Hampstead Parish Church. Just inside the side door is a bust of **(3) John Keats** presented by his American admirers.

Walk back to the front of the church and cross the road into Holly Walk with the graveyard on your right. At the end of Holly Walk, as you turn right into Mount Vernon, is Abernethy House where **(4) Robert Louis Stevenson** lived.

Follow Mount Vernon around, keeping the brick wall on your left. At the bottom of Mount Vernon, go directly ahead into Windmill Hill which is not marked until farther along. Windmill Hill winds to its end in Admiral's Walk.

Turn right into Admiral's Walk where, near the end of the walk on the left, is Grove Lodge where **(5) John Galsworthy** lived. Look back to see the Admiral's House, attached to Grove Lodge.

Before turning left into Hampstead Grove, note the house with Gothic-style windows on your right where **(6) George du Maurier** lived.

From Hampstead Grove take the first right into Upper Terrace which leads to Heath Street. Left on Heath Street to the first crosswalk. Cross and go down East Heath Road, staying on the right side of the road. Curving downhill, a little beyond where, on the opposite side, the Vale of Health road enters East Heath Road, is a tall white house, No. 17 East Heath Road where **(7) Katherine Mansfield** lived.

Double back slightly, cross East Heath Road and go down Vale of Health, which looks like a wide footpath but is in fact a road. On a stand at the bottom of the hill is a map of the cul-de-sac of the Vale of Health.

The farthest left of the first group of houses is where **(8)**
   Rabindranath Tagore lived. Facing his house, take the narrow
   flagstone path on the left side of the house. A long fence of
   woven branches will be on your left. On your right, in a row of
   cottages, is the one where **(9) Leigh Hunt** lived.

At the end of the footpath, follow right, looping back past No.1
   Byron Villas, home of **(10) D. H. Lawrence**.

Keep right past Milton Cottage and at the end of the sidewalk take
   the first narrow footpath in the grass to the left. (If you miss
   that one, there are several more to the left.) This plunge into
   the wild heath leads to the Hampstead Ponds where **(11) Percy
   Bysshe Shelley** used to sail boats.

At the end of the Hampstead Ponds, turn right on a wide footpath
   to East Heath Road again and cross the road at Well Walk, *not*
   at Well Road, which comes first. Well Walk (formerly Foley
   Avenue) is where **(12) John Keats** had lodgings (now gone) and
   where **John Masefield** lived at No.14.

Turn left on Church Hill then left onto Willow Road and keep
   straight on, continuing across Downshire Hill and into South
   End Road. To the right is a sign to Keats's House.

(Optional: At the end of Willow Road, cross Heath Road, go
   through the parking area past the sign "No Horses," and climb
   the small hill on Hampstead Heath for a view of London.)

Either turn left into Keats Grove and visit the house of **(13) John
   Keats** now or continue down South End Road, where there are
   delis and coffee bars. On the building at the corner of South
   End Road and Pond Street is a plaque and bas-relief of **(14)
   George Orwell** who worked at the bookstore formerly on this
   site and lived above it.

From Keats's House, turn left on Keats Grove, left on Downshire
   Hill, and right on Hampstead High Street to Hampstead station.

*This walk is about 2 to 2½ hours not including time for meals or tea,
or for visiting Keats's House.*

Further Reading

Boswell, James. *Boswell's London Journal.* Hammondsworth: Penguin, 1966.

Davies, Andrew. *Literary London.* London: Macmillan, 1989.

Donoghue, Denis. *William Butler Yeats.* New York: Ecco Press, 1989.

Eagle, Dorothy and Hilary Carnell, eds. *The Oxford Literary Guide to the British Isles.* Oxford: The Clarendon Press, 1977.

Edel, Leon. *Bloomsbury: A House of Lions.* New York: Avon, 1980.

_____. *Henry James. A Life.* New York: Harper & Row, 1985.

Ellmann, Richard. *Oscar Wilde.* New York: Knopf, 1988.

Fraser, Russell. *Young Shakespeare.* New York: Columbia University Press, 1988.

Gordon, Lyndall. *Eliot's New Life.* New York: Farrar, Straus, Giroux, 1988.

_____. *Virginia Woolf: A Writer's Life.* New York: Norton, 1986.

Holroyd, Michael. *Bernard Shaw.* Vol. 1, *1856-1898, The Search for Love.* New York: Random House, 1988.

Howard, Donald R. *Chaucer: His Life, His Work, His World.* New York: Dutton, 1987.

Morton, Brian N. *Americans in London: A Street by Street Guide.* New York: William Morrow, 1986.

Kaplan, Justin. *Mr. Clemens and Mark Twain.* New York: Simon and Schuster, 1983.

Tomalin, Claire. *Katherine Mansfield, A Secret Life.* New York: Knopf, 1988.

Index